AN ACCOUNT OF THE MANNER OF INOCULATING FOR THE SMALL POX IN THE EAST INDIES

AN ACCOUNT OF THE MANNER OF INOCULATING FOR THE SMALL POX IN THE EAST INDIES

JOHN ZEPHANIAH HOLWELL

ISBN: 978-93-88370-98-1

First Published: 1767

LECTOR HOUSE LLP
E-MAIL: lectorpublishing@gmail.com

AN ACCOUNT
OF THE
MANNER OF INOCULATING
FOR THE
SMALL POX IN THE EAST INDIES.

AN ACCOUNT
OF THE
MANNER OF INOCULATING
FOR THE
SMALL POX IN THE EAST INDIES.

WITH SOME
OBSERVATIONS ON THE PRACTICE
AND MODE OF TREATING THAT DISEASE IN THOSE PARTS.

INSCRIBED TO THE LEARNED
THE PRESIDENT, AND MEMBERS OF THE
COLLEGE OF PHYSICIANS IN LONDON.

BY

J. Z. HOLWELL, F. R. S.

MDCCLXVII.

AN ACCOUNT
OF THE MANNER OF
INOCULATING FOR THE SMALL POX
IN THE EAST INDIES.

On perusing lately some tracts upon the subject of Inoculation, I determined to put together a few notes relative to the manner of Inoculation, practised, time out of mind, by the Bramins of Indostan; to this I was chiefly instigated, by considering the great benefit that may arise to mankind from a knowledge of this foreign method, which so remarkably tends to support the practice now generally followed with such marvellous success. The Manner of Inoculating for the small pox

By Dr. SCHULTZ's account of Inoculation, page 65, note (9), it should seem, that the world has been already obliged with a performance of the kind which I have now undertaken, by a Dutch author, a friend of Mr. CHAIS; but as this is all I know of that work, it shall not discourage my proceeding with my own, the more especially as that performance is in a foreign language, and may not much benefit my country.

As many years are elapsed, since a theme of this nature has employed my thoughts and attention; I will hope for every favorable indulgence from the candor of that learned and respectable Body, to whose judgment I most readily submit the following history and observations.

It has been lately remarked by a learned and judicious ornament of the College of Physicians, "That the Art of Medicine has, in several instances, been greatly indebted to Accident; and that some of its most valuable improvements have been received from the hands of Ignorance and Barbarism; a Truth, remarkably exemplified in the practice of INOCULATION of the SMALL POX." — However just in general this learned Gentleman's remark may be, he will, as to his particular reference, be surprized to find, that nearly the same salutary method, now so happily pursued in England, (howsoever it has been seemingly blundered upon) has the sanction of remotest antiquity; but indeed with some variations, that will rather illustrate the propriety of the present Practice, and promote the obvious very laudable intention, with which that Gentleman published his late Essay on this interesting subject.

The general state of this distemper in the Provinces of Bengall (to which these observations are limited) is such, that for five and sometimes six years together, it passes in a manner unnoticed, from the few that are attacked with it; for the complexion of it in these years is generally so benign as to cause very little alarm; and notwithstanding the multitudes that are every year inoculated in the usual season, it adds no malignity to the disease taken in the natural way, nor spreads the infection, as is commonly imagined in Europe. Every seventh year, with scarcely any exception, the Small Pox rages epidemically in these Provinces, during the months of March, April, and May; and sometimes until the annual returning rains, about the middle of June, put a stop to its fury. On these periodical returns (to four of which I have been a witness) the disease proves universally of the most malignant confluent kind, from which few either of the natives or Europeans escaped, that took the distemper in the natural way, commonly dying on the first, second, or third day of the eruption; and yet, Inoculation in the East, has natural fears and superstitious prejudices to encounter, as well as in the West. The usual resource of the Europeans is to fly from the settlements, and retire into the country before the return of the Small Pox season.

It is singularly worth remarking, that there hardly ever was an instance of a native of the Island of St. Helena, man or woman, that was seized with this distemper in the natural way (when resident in Bengall,) who escaped with life; altho' it is a known fact the disease never yet got footing upon that Island. Clearly to account for this, is not an easy matter; I will venture, however, a few conjectures on the occasion. These people rarely migrate from the Island before they arrive at years of maturity; the basis of their diet there, from their infancy, is a root called yam, of a skranshee kind, a term they use to express its acrid, unwholesome qualities, which frequently subjects them to epidemic and dangerous dysenteries, and sometimes epidemic putrid sore throats. The blood thus charged, must necessarily constitute a most unlucky habit of body to combat with any acute inflammatory disease whatsoever, but more especially of the kind under consideration (so frequently attended with a high degree of putrefaction,) always fatal to these people, even in those seasons when the disease is mild and favorable to others: But indeed it is a general remark, that a St. Helenian rarely escapes when seized with the Small Pox in whatsoever part of the Globe he happens to reside. The same has been observed of the African Coffries, altho' I know not what cause to ascribe it to, unless we suppose one similar to that above mentioned, to wit, some fundamental aggravating principle in their chief diet. Be this as it may, that these two portions of the human species seem peculiarly marked as victims to this disease, is a fact indisputable, let the cause be what it will.

Having thus far premised touching the general state of this distemper in the Provinces of Bengall, (which I believe is nearly applicable to every other part of the Empire) I will only add a few words respecting the duration of it in Indostan, and then hasten to the principal intention of this short Essay.

The learned Doctor FREIND in his History of Physic from the time of GALEN, has this remarkable passage: "By the earliest account we have of the Small Pox, we find it first appeared in Ægypt in the time of Omar, successor to Mahomet: though no doubt, since the Greeks knew nothing of it, the Arabians brought it from their own country, and might derive it originally from some of the more distant regions of the East." The sagacity of this conclusion, later times and discoveries has fully verified; at the period in which the Aughtorrah Bhade scriptures of the Gentoos were promulged, (according to the Bramins three thousand three hundred and sixty six years ago;) this disease must then have been of some standing, as those scriptures institute a form of divine worship, with Poojahs, or offerings, to a female Divinity, stiled by the common people Gootee ka Tagooran (the Goddess of Spots,) whose aid and patronage are invoked during the continuance of the Small Pox season, also in the Measles, and every cutaneous Eruption that is in the smallest degree epidemical. Due weight being given to this circumstance, the long duration of the Disease in Indostan will manifestly appear; and we may add to the sagacious conjecture just quoted, that not only the Arabians, but the Ægyptians also, by their early commerce with India through the Red Sea and Gulf of Mocha, most certainly derived originally the Small Pox (and probably the Measles likewise) from that country, where those diseases have reigned from the earliest known times.

Inoculation is performed in Indostan by a particular tribe of Bramins, who are delegated annually for this service from the different Colleges of Bindoobund, Eleabas, Banaras, &c. over all the distant Provinces; dividing themselves into small parties, of three or four each, they plan their travelling circuits in such wise as to arrive at the places of their respective destination some weeks before the usual return of the disease; they arrive commonly in the Bengali Provinces early in February, although they some years do not begin to inoculate before March, deferring it until they consider the state of the season, and acquire information of the state of the distemper.

The year in Bengall can properly be divided into three seasons only, of four months each; from the middle of June to the middle of October is the rainy season; from the middle of October to the middle of February is the cold season, which never rises to a degree of freezing; the whole globe does not yield a more desirable or delightful climate than Bengall during these four months; but the freedom of living, which the Europeans fall into at this season, sow the seeds of those diseases which spring up in all the succeeding months of the year. From the middle of February to the middle of June is the hot, windy, dry season; during which no rain falls but what comes in storms of fierce winds and tremendous thunder and lightning, called North Westers, the quarter they always rise from; and the Provinces, particularly Bengall, is more or less healthy, in proportion to the number of these storms; when in this season the air is frequently agitated and refreshed with these North Westers, accompanied with rain, (for they are often dry,) and the inhabitants do not expose themselves to the intense sun and violent hot winds that blow in March, April, and May, it is generally found to be the most healthy of the year; otherwise (as in the year 1744, when we had no rain from the twentieth of October to the twentieth of June) this season produces high inflammatory disorders of the liver, breast, pleura, and intestines, with dysenteries, and a deplorable species of the Small-Pox.

From the middle of July (the second month of the rainy season) there is little or no wind, a stagnation of air follows, and during the remainder of this month, and the months of August and September, the atmosphere is loaded with suffocating heat and moisture, the parents of putrefaction; and nervous putrid fevers (approaching sometimes to pestilential) take the lead, and mark the dangerous season; from these fevers the Natives frequently recover, but the Europeans seldom, especially if they in the preceding May and June indulged too freely in those two *bewitching delicacies, Mangos* and *Mango Fish*, indiscriminately with the free use of *flesh* and *wine*; for these (*all together*) load the whole habit with impurities, and never fail of yielding Death a plentiful harvest, in the three last months of this putrid season: If any are seized with the Small-Pox in these months, it is ever of the most malignant kind, and usually fatal. It will not, I hope, be deemed a useless digression, if I bestow a few remarks on the nature of this *Bengall Fever*.

A day or two before the seizure, the patient finds his appetite fall off, feels an unaccountable lassitude, and failure in the natural moisture of the mouth, is low spirited without any apparent cause, and cannot sleep as usual; but having no acute complaint whatsoever, nor preternatural heat, that should indicate a fever, he attributes the whole to the heat of the season, is satisfied with fasting and confinement to his house, or goes abroad amongst his friends to "shake it off," as the common phrase is; but on the third day, finding every one of these symptoms increase, he begins to think something is really the matter with him, and the Physician is called in: thus the only period is lost wherein art might be of any use; for in the course of eighteen years practice I never knew an instance of recovery from this genuine fever, where the first three days had elapsed without assistance, and the patient in this case dyed on the fifth or seventh day. In some, this fever is attended with a full, equal, undisturbed pulse, but obviously greatly oppressed; in others, with a low and depressed one, but equal and undisturbed also, and yet both required the same treatment. New comers in the profession, have been often fatally misled by the full pulse, which they thought indicated the loss of blood; they followed the suggestion, the pulse suddenly fell, and when that happens from this cause, the art of man can never raise it again, the patient dies on the fifth or seventh day; and the consequence was exactly the same, if Nature, being overloaded, attempted to free herself of part of the burden by a natural hæmorrhage, or by the intestines, on the second or third day, (which I have often seen) they proved equally fatal as the launcet. Until the close of the sixth day the skin and urine preserved a natural state; but if at this period of the fever the skin suddenly acquired an intense heat, and the urine grew crude and limpid, it was a sure presage of death on the seventh. The natural crisis of this fever, when attacked in the very beginning, and treated judiciously, was regularly on the eleventh day, and appeared in a multitude of small boils, chiefly upon the head, or in small watery bladders thrown out upon the surface of the skin, but in the greatest abundance on the breast, neck, throat, and forehead; both of these critical appearances are constantly preceded, on the tenth day, by a copious sediment and separation in the urine. If by any inadvertent exposure to the cold air, these critical eruptions were struck in, the repelled matter instantly fell upon the brain, and convulsions and death followed in a few hours, and small purple spots remained in the places of the eruptions. Such is the genuine putrid nervous fever of Bengall, which never gave way properly to any treatment but that of blisters applied universally, supported by the strongest alexipharmics: sometimes I have seen the crisis (by unskilful management) spun out to the twenty-first day, but it has been ever imperfect, and the patient is harrassed with intermittents or diarrhœas, and commonly dies in the beginning of the cold season; but if he is of a strong constitution, he lingers on, in a dying way, until the month of February, which usually gives some turn in his favor, but his health is hardly ever re-established before the salutary mango season, which fruit, eaten with milk, proves an effectual and never-failing restorative. But to resume our subject.

The inhabitants of Bengall, knowing the usual time when the Inoculating Bramins annually return, observe strictly the regimen enjoined, whether they determine to be inoculated or not; this preparation consists only in abstaining for a month from fish, milk, and ghee, (a kind of butter made generally of buffalo's milk;) the prohibition of fish respects only the native Portuguese and Mahomedans, who abound in every Province of the Empire.

When the Bramins begin to Inoculate, they pass from house to house and operate at the door, refusing to inoculate any who have not, on a strict scrutiny, duly observed the preparatory course enjoined them. It is no uncommon thing for them to ask the Parents how many Pocks they chuse their Children should have: Vanity, we should think, urged a question on a matter seemingly so uncertain in the issue; but true it is, that they hardly ever exceed, or are deficient, in the number required.

They inoculate indifferently on any part, but if left to their choice, they prefer the outside of the arm, mid-way between the wrist and the elbow, for the males; and the same between the elbow and the shoulder for the females. Previous to the operation the Operator takes a piece of cloth in his hand, (which becomes his perquisite if the family is opulent,) and with it gives a dry friction upon the part intended for Inoculation, for the space of eight or ten minutes, then with a small instrument he wounds, by many slight touches, about the compass of a silver groat[1], just making the smallest appearance of blood, then opening a linen double

[1] The instrument they make use of, is of iron, about four inches and a half long, and of the size of a large crow quill, the middle is twisted, and the one end is steeled and flatted about an inch from the extremity, and the eighth of an inch broad; this extremity is brought to a very keen edge, and two sharp corners; the other end of the instrument is an ear-picker, and the instrument is precisely the same as the Barbers of Indostan use to cut the nails, and depurate the ears of their customers, (for in that country, we are above performing either or these operations ourselves.) The Operator of Inoculation holds the instrument as we hold a pen, and with dextrous expedition gives about fifteen or sixteen minute scarifications (within the compass abovementioned) with one of the sharp corners of the instrument, and to these various little wounds, I believe may be ascribed the discharge which almost constantly flows from the part in the progress of the disease. I cannot help thinking that too much has been said (pro and con) about nothing, respecting the different methods preferred by different Practitioners of performing the operation; provided the matter is thrown into the blood, it is certainly a consideration of most trivial import by what means it is effected; if any claims a preference, I should conclude it should be that method which bids fairest for

rag (which he always keeps in a cloth round his waist) takes from thence a small pledgit of cotton charged with the variolous matter, which he moistens with two or three drops of the *Ganges* water, and applies it to the wound, fixing it on with a slight bandage, and ordering it to remain on for six hours without being moved, then the bandage to be taken off, and the pledget to remain until it falls off itself; sometimes (but rarely) he squeezes a drop from the pledget, upon the part, before he applies it; from the time he begins the dry-friction, to the tying the knot of the bandage, he never ceases reciting some portions of the worship appointed, by the *Aughtorrah Bhade*, to be paid to the female Divinity before-mentioned, nor quits the most solemn countenance all the while. The cotton, which he preserves in a double callico rag, is saturated with matter from the inoculated pustules of the preceding year, for they never inoculate with fresh matter, nor with matter from the disease caught in the natural way, however distinct and mild the species. He then proceeds to give instructions for the treatment of the patient through the course of the process, which are most religiously observed; these are as follow:

He extends the prohibition of fish, milk, and ghee, for one month from the day of Inoculation; early on the morning succeeding the operation, four collons (an earthen pot containing about two gallons) of cold water are ordered to be thrown over the patient, from the head downwards, and to be repeated every morning and evening until the fever comes on, (which usually is about the close of the sixth day from the Inoculation,) then to desist until the appearance of the eruptions, (which commonly happens at the close of the third complete day from the commencement of the fever,) and then to pursue the cold bathing as before, through the course of the disease, and until the scabs of the pustules drop off. They are ordered to open all the pustules with a fine sharp pointed thorn, as soon as they begin to change their colour, and whilst the matter continues in a fluid state. Confinement to the house is absolutely forbid, and the inoculated are ordered to be exposed to every air that blows; and the utmost indulgence they are allowed when the fever comes on, is to be laid on a mat at the door; but, in fact, the eruptive fever is generally so inconsiderable and trifling, as very seldom to require this indulgence. Their regimen is ordered to consist of all the refrigerating things the climate and season produces, as plantains, sugar-canes, water-melons, rice, gruel made of white poppy-seeds, and cold water, or thin rice gruel for their ordinary drink. These instructions being given, and an injunction laid on the patients to make a thanksgiving *Poojah*, or Offering, to the Goddess on their recovery, the Operator takes his fee, which from the poor is a *pund of cowries*, equal to about a penny sterling, and goes on to another door, down one side of the street and up on the other, and is thus employed from morning until night, inoculating sometimes eight or ten in a house. The regimen they order, when they are called to attend the disease taken in the natural way, is uniformly the same. There usually begins to be a discharge from the scarification a day before the eruption, which continues through the disease, and sometimes after the scabs of the Pock fall off, and a few pustules generally appear round the edge of the wound; when these two circumstances appear only, without a single eruption on any other part of the body, the patient is <u>deemed as secure from future infection, as if the eruption had be</u>en general.
securing a plentiful discharge from the ulcer.

When the before recited treatment of the Inoculated is strictly followed, it is next to a miracle to hear, that one in a million fails of receiving the infection, or of one that miscarries under it; of the multitudes I have seen inoculated in that country, the number of pustules have been seldom less than fifty, and hardly ever exceeded two hundred. Since, therefore, this practice of the East has been followed without variation, and with uniform success from the remotest known times, it is but justice to conclude, it must have been originally founded on the basis of rational principles and experiment.

Although I was very early prejudiced in preference of the cool regimen and free admission of air, in the treatment of this disease, yet, on my arrival in Bengall, I thought the practice of the Bramins carried both to a bold, rash, and dangerous extreme; but a few years experience gave me full conviction of the propriety of their method: this influenced my practice, and the success was adequate; and I will venture to say, that every gentleman in the Profession who did not adopt the same mode, (making a necessary distinction and allowance between the constitutions of the Natives and Europeans,) have lost many a patient, which might otherwise have been saved; as I could prove in many instances, where I have been called in too late to be of any assistance. But to form a judgment of the propriety of this Eastern practice with more precision, it will be best to analyze it, from the period of the enjoined preparation, to the end of the process; as thereby an opportunity presents itself of displaying the principles on which the Bramins act, and by which they justify their singular method of practice.

It has been already said, that the preparative course consists only in abstaining from fish, milk, and ghee; respecting the first, it is known to be a viscid and inflammatory diet, tending to foul and obstruct the cutaneous glands and excretory ducts, and to create in the stomach and first passages a tough, slimy phlegm, highly injurious to the human constitution; as these are the generally supposed qualities of this diet, it seems forbid upon the justest grounds.

Touching milk, which is the basis (next to rice) of all the natives food, I confess I was surprized to find it one of the forbidden articles, until I was made acquainted with their reasoning on the subject. They say that milk becomes highly nutritious, not only from its natural qualities, but principally from its ready admission into the blood, and quick assimulation with it; and that it consequently is a warm heating diet, and must have a remote tendency to inflammation, whenever the blood is thrown into any preternatural ferment, and therefore, that milk is a food highly improper, at a season when the preternatural fermentation that produces the Small Pox ought to be feared, and guarded against by every person who knows himself liable to the disease, or determined to prepare himself for receiving it, either from nature or art. Upon this principle and reasoning it is, that their women, during the course of their periodical visitations, are strictly forbid, and religiously abstain from, the use of milk, lest it should, upon any accidental cold, dispose the uterus to inflammation and ulceration; and from the same apprehension, the use of it is as strictly prohibited during the flow of the lochia, and is avoided as so much poison; our European women, resident in India, have adopted the same precaution from experience of the effect, and will not, on any consideration, at those times, mix the smallest quantity with their tea, a lesson they derive from their Midwives, who are all natives, and generally are instructed in their calling by the Bramins, and other Practitioners in Physic.

Concerning the third interdicted article, they allege, that under *that* is implied a prohibition of all fat and oily substances, as their qualities are nearly similar with those of fish, and similar in their effects of fouling the first passages in a high degree above any other aliment that is taken into them; that they soon acquire an acrimony in the course of digestion, and convey the same into the blood and juices; these premises being granted, which I think can hardly be denied, there appears sufficient cause for prohibiting the use of the whole tribe; the more especially, as ghee and oil are the essential ingredients used in cooking their vegetable diet.

Thus far the system of practice pursued by the Bramins will, I imagine, appear rational enough, and well founded; but they have other reasons for particularly prohibiting the use of these three articles, which to some may appear purely speculative, if not chimerical. They lay it down as a principle, that the immediate (or instant) cause of the Small Pox exists in the mortal part of every human and animal form[2]; that the mediate (or second) acting cause, which stirs up the first, and throws it into a state of fermentation, is multitudes of imperceptible animalculæ floating in the atmosphere; that these are the cause of all epidemical diseases, but more particularly of the Small Pox; that they return at particular seasons in greater or lesser numbers; that these bodies, imperceptible as they are to the human organs of vision, imprison the most malignant tribes of the fallen angelic Spirits: That these animalculæ touch and adhere to every thing, in greater or lesser proportions, according to the nature of the surfaces which they encounter; that they pass and repass in and out of the bodies of all animals in the act of respiration, without injury to themselves, or the bodies they pass through; that such is not the case with those that are taken in with the food, which, by mastication, and the digestive faculties of the stomach and intestines, are crushed and assimulated with the chyle, and conveyed into the blood, where, in a certain time, their malignant juices excite a fermentation peculiar to the immediate (or instant) cause, which ends in an eruption on the skin. That they adhere more closely, and in greater numbers, to glutinous, fat, and oily substances, by which they are in a manner taken prisoners; that fish, milk, and ghee, have these qualities in a more eminent and dangerous degree, and attach the animalculæ, and convey them in greater quantities into the blood; and for these reasons, added to those before assigned, they are forbid to be taken in food during the preparative course. They add, that the Small Pox is more or

[2] In an epidemic season of the confluent Small Pox, Turkeys, Chittygong Fowls, Madrass Capons, and other poultry, are carried off by the disease in great numbers; and have the symptoms usually accompanying every stage of the distemper. I had a favourite Parrot that died of it in the year 1744; in him I had a fair opportunity of observing the regular progress of the disorder; he sickened, and had an ardent fever full two days before the eruption, and died on the seventh day of the eruption; on opening him, we found his throat, stomach, and whole channel of the first passages, lined as thick with the pustules as the surface of his body, where, for the most part, they rose contiguous, but in other places they ran together.

less epidemical, more mild or malignant, in proportion as the air is charged with these animalculæ, and the quantity of them received with the food. That though we all receive, with our aliment, a portion of them, yet it is not always sufficient in quantity to raise this peculiar ferment, and yet may be equal to setting the seeds of other diseases in motion; hence the reason why any epidemical disorder seldom appears alone. That when once this peculiar ferment, which produces the Small Pox, is raised in the blood, the immediate (instant) cause of the disease is totally expelled in the eruptions, or by other channels; and hence it is, that the blood is not susceptible of a second fermentation of the same kind. That Inoculating for this disease was originally hinted by the Divinity presiding over the immediate (instant) cause, the thought being much above the reach of human wisdom and foresight. That the great and obvious benefit accruing from it, consists in this, that the fermentation being excited by the action of a small portion of matter (similar to the immediate cause) which had already passed through a state of fermentation, the effects must be moderate and benign; whereas the fermentation raised by the malignant juices of the animalculæ received into the blood with the aliment, gives necessarily additional force and strength to the first efficient cause of the disease.

That noxious animalculæ, floating in the atmosphere, are the cause of all pestilential, and other epidemical disorders, is a doctrine the Bramins are not singular in; however, some of the conclusions drawn from it, are purely their own. A speculative genius may amuse itself by assigning this or that efficient cause, or first principle of this disease; but the best conjecture which the wisdom of man can frame, will appear vague and uncertain; nor is it of much moment, in the present case, to puzzle the imagination, by a minute enquiry into the essence of a cause hidden from us, when the effects are so visible, and chiefly call for our regard: but if we must assign *a cause*, why every part of the globe, *at particular seasons*, is more liable to peculiar malignant epidemical diseases, than *at others*, (which experience manifests) I see no one that so much wears the complexion of probability, as that of pestilent animalculæ, driven by stated winds, or generated on the spot by water and air in a state of stagnation, (and consequently in a state of putrefaction favourable to their propagation,) and received into the habit with our food and respiration. We yearly see, in a greater or lesser degree, the baneful effects of these insects in blights, although at their first seizure of a plant they are invisible, even with the assistance of the best glasses; and I hope I shall not be thought to refine too much on the argument, if I give it as my opinion, that epidemical blights, and epidemical diseases of one kind or other, may be observed to go often hand in hand with each other, from the same identical cause. But to proceed in our analysis.

The mode by which the Eastern Inoculators convey the variolous taint into the blood, has nothing uncommon in it, unless we except the preceding friction upon the part intended for Inoculation, and moistening the saturated pledget, before the application of it; for this practice they alledge the following reasons; that by friction the circulation in the small sanguinary vessels is accelerated, and the matter being diluted by a small portion of Ganges water, is, from both causes, more readily and eagerly received, and the operation at the same time sanctified. The friction and dilution of the matter, has certainly the sanction of very good common sense; and the Ganges water, I doubt not, may have as much efficacy as any other holy water whatsoever. This last circumstance, however, keeps up the piety and solemnity with which the operation is conducted from the beginning to the end of it; it tends also to give confidence to the patient, and so far is very laudable. The reasons they assign for giving the preference to matter of the preceding year, are singular and judicious; they urge, it is more certain in its effects; that necessity first pointed out the fact, (the variolous matter some years not being procurable,) and experience confirmed it: they add, that when the matter is effectually secured from the air, it undergoes at the return of the season an imperceptible fermentation, which gives fresh vigour to its action. It is no uncommon thing to inoculate with matter four or five years old, but they generally prefer that of a year old, conceiving that the fermentation which constitutes its superiority over fresh matter, is yearly lessened, and consequently the essential spirit of action weakened, after the first year.

The next article of the Eastern practice, which offers in the course of our discussion, is their sluicing their patients over head and ears, morning and evening, with cold water, until the fever comes on; in which the inoculating Bramins are, beyond controversy, singular: but before we can penetrate the grounds and reasons for this practice, it becomes necessary to bestow a few words on the usual manner of cold bathing in the East, when medically applied, which is simply this; the water is taken up over night, in three, four, or five vessels, before described, (according to the strength of the patient,) and left in the open air, to receive the dews of the night, which gives it an intense coldness; then in the morning, before the sun rises, the water is poured without intermission, by two servants, over the body, from the distance of six or twelve inches above the head. This mode of cold bathing has been adopted from the Eastern professors of Physic, by all the European practitioners, and by constant experience found abundantly more efficacious than that by immersion, in all cases where that very capital remedy was indicated; notwithstanding it has been ever the received opinion, that the success of cold bathing, is as much, or rather more, owing to the weight and pressure of the circumambient body of water, than the shock. The remarkable superior efficacy of this Eastern method of cold bathing, can only be accounted for, from the shock being infinitely greater, and of longer continuance, than that received by immersion; which is a fact indisputable, as will be acknowledged by every one who goes through a course of both methods; the severity of the one being nothing comparable to the other: this I assert from my own personal feelings; and I never had a patient that did not aver the same, who had undergone both trials: indeed, the shock of this Eastern method is so great, that, in many cases, when the subject was deeply exhausted and relaxed, I have found it absolutely necessary to begin the course only with a quart of water.

If the known effects of cold bathing are attended to, and its sovereign virtues duly considered, in the very different circumstances of Palsies, Rheumatisms, general relaxation of the solids, and particular relaxation of the stomach and intestines, we shall not be long at a loss to account for this part of the Eastern practice in the course of Inoculation: They allege in defence of it, that by the sudden shock of the cold water, and consequent increased motion of the blood, all offensive principles are forcibly driven from the heart, brain, and other interior parts of the body, towards the extremities and surface, and at the same time the intended fermentation is thereby more speedily and certainly promoted; (hence it probably is, that the fever generally commences so early as about the close of the sixth day.) When the fever appears, they desist from the use of the cold water, because when the fermentation is once begun, the blood should not, they say, receive any additional commotion until the eruption appears, when they again resume the cold water, and continue it to the end of the disease; asserting, that the use of it alone, by the daily fresh impetus it gives to the blood, enables it utterly to expel and drive out the remainder of the immediate cause of the disease into the pustules. I have been myself an eye-witness to many instances of its marvelous effect, where the pustules have sunk, and the patient appeared in imminent danger, but almost instantly restored by the application of three or four collans of cold water, which never fails of filling the Pock, as it were by enchantment; and so great is the stress laid by the Eastern Practitioners on this preparative, (for as the three interdicted articles in food is preparative to the Inoculation, so this may be deemed preparative to the eruption,) that when they are called in, and find, upon enquiry, that circumstance (and opening the pustules) has not been attended to, they refuse any further attendance.

The next and last article of the Eastern practice, which falls under our consideration, is that just abovementioned, viz. the opening of the Pustules, whilst the matter continues in a fluid state. That a circumstance so important, so self-evidently rational and essential, should have been so long unthought of, appears most wonderful! and if my memory fails me not, HELVETIUS is the only writer upon the subject of the Small Pox, that hinted it in practice before Doctor TISSOT; this accurate and benevolent Physician has enforced it with such strength of judgment and argument, that he leaves little room (except facts) to add to his pathetic persuasive; in this he is supported by his learned and elegant Commentator and Translator Doctor KIRKPATRICK, (page 226 and 227,) and I am not without hopes it will, contrary to Doctor TISSOT's expectation, "become a general practice;" the more especially, when it is found to have invariable success, and venerable antiquity, for its sanction.

So great is the dependence which the Eastern Practitioners have on opening the Pustules, in every malignant kind of the disease, that where the fluid state of the matter has been suffered to elapse without being evacuated, they pronounce the issue fatal, and it generally proves so; they order it in every kind, even the most distinct; for although in these it should seem scarcely necessary, yet they conceive it effectually prevents inflammation and weakness of the eyes, biles, and other eruptions and disorders, which so commonly succeed the disease, however benign; in very critical cases, they will not trust the operation of opening the Pustules to the nurses or relations, but engage in it themselves, with amazing patience and solicitude; and I have frequently known them thus employed for many hours together; and when it has been zealously persevered in, I hardly ever knew it fail, of either intirely preventing the second fever, or mitigating it in such sort, as to render it of no consequence; in various instances, which I have been a witness to, in my own, and others practice, I have seen the Pustules in the contiguous kind, upon being successively opened, fill again to the fourth and fifth, and in the confluent, to the sixth, seventh, and eighth time; in the very distinct sort they will not fill again more than once or twice, and sometimes not at all, which was a plain indication, that the whole virus of the disease was excelled in the first eruption.

The Eastern Practitioners, with great modesty, arraign the European practice of Phlebotomy and Cathartics in any stage of the disease, but more particularly when designed to prevent, or mitigate the second fever; alledging, that the *first* weakens the natural powers, and that the *latter* counteracts the regular course of *nature*, which in this disease invariably tends to throw out the offending cause *upon the skin*; that she often proves unequal to the intire expulsion of the enemy, in which case, her wise purposes are to be assisted by art, in that track, which she herself points out, and not by a diversion of the usual crisis into another chanel; that this assistance can only be attempted with propriety, by emptying the Pustules, as thereby fresh room is given in them for the reception of the circulating matter still remaining in the blood, and which could not be contained in the first eruption; by which means every end and purpose of averting, or subduing the *second fever* is obtained, with a moral certainty; whilst Phlebotomy and Cathartics, administered with this view, are both irrational and precarious; as being opposite to the constant operation of Nature in her management of this dreadful disease.

It remains only that I add a word or two upon the Eastern manner of opening the Pustules, which (as before mentioned) is directed to be done with a very fine sharp pointed thorn: Experience has established the use of this natural instrument in preference to either the scissars, launcet, or needle; the Practitioners perforate the most prominent part of the Pustule, and with the sides of the thorn press out the pus; and having opened about a dozen, they absorb the matter with a callico rag, dipt in warm water and milk; and proceed thus until the whole are discharged: the orifice made by the thorn is so extremely small, that it closes immediately after the matter is pressed out, so that there is no admission of the external air into the Pustule, which would suddenly contract the mouths of the excretory vessels, and consequently the further secretion of the variolous matter from the blood would be thereby obstructed; for this consideration, the method recommended by Doctor TISSOT, of clipping the Pustules with sharp pointed scissars, is certainly liable to objection, as the aperture would be too large; when in the true confluent kind, no distinct Pustules present, they perforate the most prominent and promising parts, in many places, at the distance of a tenth of an inch, usually beginning at the extremities; and I have often seen the Pustules in the *contiguous*, and the perforated parts in the *confluent* kind, fill again before the operation has been half over; yet they do not repeat the opening until a few hours elapse, conceiving it proper that the matter should receive some degree of concoction in the Pustules before it is again discharged.

If the foregoing Essay on the Eastern mode of treating the Small Pox, throws any new and beneficial lights upon this cruel and destructive disease, or leads to support and confirm the present successful and happy method of Inoculation, in such wise as to introduce, into *regular and universal practice, the cool regimen and free admission of Air,* (the contrary having proved the bane of millions,) I shall, in either case, think the small time and trouble bestowed in putting these facts together most amply recompensed.

Chilton Lodge, Wilts,
September 1, 1767.

FINIS.

Lector House believes that a society develops through a two-fold approach of continuous learning and adaptation, which is derived from the study of classic literary works spread across the historic timeline of literature records. Therefore, we aim at reviving, repairing and redeveloping all those inaccessible or damaged but historically as well as culturally important literature across subjects so that the future generations may have an opportunity to study and learn from past works to embark upon a journey of creating a better future.

This book is a result of an effort made by Lector House towards making a contribution to the preservation and repair of original ancient works which might hold historical significance to the approach of continuous learning across subjects.

HAPPY READING & LEARNING!

LECTOR HOUSE LLP
E-MAIL: lectorpublishing@gmail.com